# Modernising Legacy Applications

# in the Public Sector

Written by
Luke Morton and David Winter
of Made Tech

ISBN: 9798675015979

First Printing: August 2020

www.madetech.com

Illustrations by Alexi McCarthy

# Acknowledgments

A special mention to Rory MacDonald, Ben Pirt and Joe Carstairs for helping out with this book.

We would also like to thank everyone who has provided feedback on the book content, especially Chad Bond, Dave Rogers and James Stewart.

# Contents

# Preface

Legacy technology is one of the biggest threats to public sector organisations.

From reputational damage to loss of life, the risk of doing nothing is so great that this issue needs to be tackled urgently. It is of pressing importance to those directing public sector technology too, with the House of Commons Select Committee for Science and Technology having directed the Government Digital Service (GDS) to conduct an audit of all legacy systems across government before the end of 2020.

So what should Digital, Data and Technology leaders do?

Most are well aware of at least one area of legacy technology that poses a risk but the reasons for it not being addressed are never the same for each organisation. It might be that funding hasn't been directed towards modernising legacy applications. Or that an application has been left untouched for so long that no-one dares make a change in case it breaks a critical service for citizens.

Modernising legacy applications starts with understanding the risks and drivers that are unique to your organisation. Then it's about building the right team for the job so that the full range of internal and external users are considered and designed for.

Crucially, leaders need to understand how they might achieve transformation for their organisations. They need to know how to map their organisation and their application ecosystem so they can choose which ones to prioritise. Then they need to understand which transformation strategies exist and how they can be implemented successfully in order to solve legacy issues and start building sustainable technology in the future.

This is what modernising legacy applications is all about.

# Who is this book for?

This book is for Digital, Data and technology leaders, including Chief Digital Officers, Chief Technology Officers, Chief Information Officers and Directors of IT.

You may have already identified a legacy technology risk in your organisation and be working on how to solve it. You may have had to design your processes around your legacy systems to the detriment of your staff and the citizens you serve. You may simply be aware that an application has been left untouched for so long that it is becoming riskier by the day.

Whether you've started your journey already or don't know where to begin, this book is for forward thinking leaders who want to deliver sustainable technology by making legacy applications a thing of the past.

# How can it help me?

This book has been written to guide you through the steps you need to take to modernise your legacy applications. While every organisation is different, it can help any Digital, Data and Technology leader because it empowers you to define and implement the right approach for your organisation.

For those of you at the very start of your journey, this means helping you to understand the risks your legacy applications pose and the drivers for transformation in your organisation. From here, the book describes the initial steps to ensure your transformation is a success, including accessing finance and building the right team.

Then, the book will help you to prioritise your transformation by explaining the organisational and application mapping that needs to take place. Once you've researched the problem, you need to know what can be done to solve it, which is why a large portion of the book is dedicated to explaining the different strategies for modernising legacy applications and how to implement them.

Finally, the book looks to the future and how you can maintain the positive changes you've made in order to continue building sustainable technology from now on.

# CHAPTER 1.1
# THE PITFALLS OF
# NEGLECTING LEGACY APPLICATION
# TRANSFORMATION

Legacy technology is a huge threat to the public sector. While this won't be the first time you've read this, it remains relevant because not enough action is being taken to prevent disaster.

In July 2019, the House of Commons Select Committee for Science and Technology stated that "legacy systems are a significant barrier to effective Government transformation and digitisation"[1]. It went on to say that the Government Digital Service (GDS) should conduct an audit of all legacy systems across government and that this should be completed no later than December 2020.

This urgency should be welcomed. Legacy issues need to be identified as soon as possible, and public sector leaders across digital and technology must take responsibility for highlighting the specific risks that exist in their organisations. Then they need to develop appropriate strategies for transforming their legacy applications, which are funded properly and can be executed successfully.

---

[1]
https://publications.parliament.uk/pa/cm201719/cmselect/cmsctech/1455/145510.htm

If they do not, recent examples from the private sector show us that the effects can be widespread and, in the worst cases, tragic.

# Reputational damage at British Airways

The airline has been hit by a string of IT issues in recent years, including a major data breach in 2017. However, it was the glitch in its check-in and departure systems[2] that exposed the company's flawed legacy technology strategy.

In August 2019, more than 100 flights were cancelled and 200 delayed, affecting tens of thousands of customers. While the company has been reticent about explaining why the issue occurred, some have speculated that it came down to building new service capabilities while ignoring core legacy systems.

As layers and layers of new technology are built up, it becomes harder and harder to check transaction chains across these layers and to foresee how changes in one might affect the operation of another.

---

[2] https://www.ft.com/content/f639ee04-b9f1-11e9-96bd-8e884d3ea203

# Life savings lost at TSB

In April 2018, customers of TSB experienced the first few days of what would become several weeks of significant disruptions to their banking experience. Many were unable to access their accounts. Some could see other customers' accounts or were presented with large negative balances when they tried to view their own.

In June 2018, the bank admitted that 1,300 customers had been hit by fraud, with some having their life savings stolen. These issues all came about because of the poorly executed migration of account data from legacy systems at the bank's previous owner, Lloyds, to the systems of its new owner, Sabadell.

TSB had taken the correct first step by identifying the bank's change of ownership as a key driver of legacy transformation. However, in aiming for a big bang transformation rather than ongoing incremental change [3], it clearly failed to execute in a way that derisked the impact for its customers.

---

[3]

https://medium.com/@JonHall_/lessons-from-the-tsb-failure-a-perfect-storm-of-waterfall-failures-4f4d2e789b35

# Personal tragedy at Boeing

Between October 2018 and March 2019, the US aerospace giant experienced two disastrous plane crashes, which had their roots in a policy of choosing financial restraint over legacy transformation.

Investigations into both crashes have shown that the company's decision to choose a software workaround, rather than make expensive changes to its legacy design, was at the heart of the problem. Boeing had decided to fit a bigger, more efficient engine which affected the angle of ascent during takeoff. Rather than fix how the new engine affected the plane by redesigning the build of the aeroplane though, it implemented a software workaround as a cheaper, quicker alternative.

While it must be noted that a lack of training and communication about how the new software worked also played its part in the crashes, there's no doubt that choosing to avoid large legacy transformation costs played a significant role too.

## Public sector beware

The key lessons that public sector leaders should take from these private sector examples is that failing to address, finance and implement a legacy transformation programme is very risky. Furthermore, they should be fully aware of how failing to deal with legacy technology in highly-sensitive areas of the public sector could blow up into headline-grabbing events that rival the Boeing tragedies.

But Digital and Technology leaders don't need to be shocked into action. Simply paying attention to the issues that their users experience every day should make them realise that action is required. For example, it is already clear that issues caused by legacy technology are wasting vast amounts of time for people working in some of the most important areas of the public sector.

## Legacy issues abound

At the end of 2019, it was revealed that doctors in a Midlands GPs surgery take 17 minutes to log in[4] to

---

4

https://www.telegraph.co.uk/news/2019/10/24/nhs-technology-bad-takes-17-minutes-log-pc-countrys-senior-doctor/

their computer systems in the morning. Why? Because they are forced to use legacy technology in the shape of Windows 7, for which Microsoft no longer provides technical support. Ongoing login issues are just the tip of the iceberg when it comes to the problems of legacy software though.

Looking back to May 2017, the NHS was one of many organisations across the world hit by the WannaCry ransomware attack. As a result, 34 trusts were infected and locked out of devices. Almost 600 GP practices were infected and NHS England estimated that as many as 19,000 appointments[5] would have been cancelled as a result of the attack.

All of the NHS organisations infected by WannaCry shared the same vulnerability. Like the slow login issue for the Midlands GP surgery, it relates to a reliance on legacy technology. However, in the case of WannaCry, the issue related to the use of unpatched or unsupported Windows operating systems.

In other areas of the public sector, where modernisation has been attempted, poor execution has led to relatively new digital services quickly becoming

---

[5] https://www.nao.org.uk/report/investigation-wannacry-cyber-attack-and-the-nhs/

legacy ones. In the case of the Legal Aid Agency, its Client and Cost Management System was rolled out for all civil legal aid work in April 2016 but was then described by the Legal Aid Practitioners Group as having problems 'at every level'[6] less than a year later.

To avoid new services becoming legacy services almost overnight, organisations should be aiming to build universally accessible and interoperable web applications in an incremental and derisked manner.

## Legacy AI?

When you consider critical healthcare, nuclear energy or air traffic control systems, it doesn't take a huge leap of the imagination to see how legacy issues in these areas could have tragic consequences.

One less obvious but not less significant topic to consider though is how the increasing interest in Artificial Intelligence (AI) and Machine Learning (ML) for automating decisions might be affected by legacy technology. After all, just imagine the potentially disastrous effects in 20 years' time if an AI algorithm is making benefits decisions or determining who should

---

[6]

https://www.lag.org.uk/article/201748/ccms--despair-at-a-system-unfit-for-purpose

enter the country, based on a crumbling legacy technology and data infrastructure.

We have already seen the biggest technology company in the world launch a new financial product to much fanfare only to find its AI algorithm is discriminating against women[7]. This should serve as a stark reminder to all public sector organisations that they must invest in fixing the fundamentals before they are tempted to develop a headline-grabbing AI algorithm that is built on shaky foundations.

## Taking action in your organisation

The time when legacy application transformation in the public sector could be kicked down the road has passed. GDS, NHSX and the Science and Technology Select Committee have all made it clear that this major risk needs to be addressed urgently.

The responsibility for acting falls on Digital and Technology leaders but no one should expect a quick fix. Legacy transformation takes time and requires a series of significant steps to be taken, which all require support from board level.

---

[7] https://www.bbc.co.uk/news/business-50365609

The most pragmatic first step is to look at the drivers of legacy transformation for your organisation. This will not only help your colleagues to understand the urgency of this work but also to start you on the path to developing a strategy that meets your specific needs.

# — CHAPTER 1.2 —

# WHICH FACTORS DRIVE LEGACY TRANSFORMATION IN PUBLIC SECTOR ORGANISATIONS?

CYBER SECURITY
RISKS

STREAM LINING
COSTS

MAINTAINABILITY

LEADERSHIP
CHANGES

USER
NEEDS

SKILLS
SHORTAGES

The risks of neglecting legacy transformation include everything from reputational damage to loss of life. However, trying to predict exactly what will happen to a particular public sector organisation if it ignores these risks is extremely difficult.

A more pragmatic approach is to start by identifying the drivers of legacy transformation and deciding which are the most pressing for you. Changes to legacy systems across the public sector are almost inevitable, given the significance that bodies like the Government Digital Service (GDS) have placed on change. Therefore digital and technology leaders need to act now to identify these drivers as a critical first step towards transformation.

One thing that should be front of mind from the beginning is cost. It is an outcome of almost all the other factors driving change and is an undeniably important consideration throughout any transformation process.

## Cyber security risks

The Government regards certain areas of the public sector as critical national infrastructure, with protection of the IT networks, data and systems in these areas falling under the remit of the National Cyber Security Centre.

Hackers are attracted to nearly all levels of government infrastructure as they regard them as treasure troves of sensitive information. Conscious of the major reputational damage that would be caused by a breach, digital and technology leaders have adopted the mantra of "reducing risk" wherever and whenever possible. As a result, these systems have become more and more locked down and more and more difficult to work with.

There is also the issue of how cyber security audits take place. Over time, they have been systemised into a rubber stamping process rather than a practical, collaborative exercise that helps engineers to embed security into their processes from the start. Rather than developing software, have it audited six months later and potentially roll back with fixes, engineers need to be helped to 'shift left with security' and build secure software from the start.

## Maintainability issues

One of the consequences of locking away legacy systems is that they become harder to maintain because the skills, documentation and knowledge required to keep them up-to-date disappear.

But maintainability is a driver of transformation for legacy applications that aren't considered critical too. The programming languages your apps are written in can become out-of-date simply through a lack of ongoing upkeep, to the point where it's not unusual to see language stacks in public sector organisations that haven't been updated for ten years.

As this happens, more and more security issues occur that can't be patched easily because the language or operating system is no longer supported. Where out-of-license software is still being used, organisations need to make custom (read 'expensive') arrangements with software providers to patch security issues or make changes.

These 'ransom contracts', where public sector organisations are locked-in to paying whatever a single vendor demands, are still worryingly common. Furthermore, their existence is a clear warning sign that legacy technology is an issue within an organisation.

Complacency can quickly become an issue for leaders who see maintainability decreasing but do nothing about it. If you don't transform, you will start to see a snowball effect, with issues occurring across multiple layers, from network infrastructure, across operating systems and languages.

Technical debt needs to be paid off regularly before it gets out of hand. Regular updates, at least every three months, are needed if an organisation wants to avoid getting into a situation where they have no choice but to sign expensive ransom contracts or hire engineers with niche, legacy skills to make changes.

## Meeting user needs

One of the most important drivers of legacy transformation is government policy being changed and technology not being able to keep up. This results in organisations experiencing a tension between the desire to serve users and the inability of existing systems to meet these demands.

New or evolved policy usually necessitates a change to existing systems. However, the desired change to a service journey can be blocked immediately if the underlying technology that powers it has been outsourced to a third party or left untouched for so long that no-one knows how to make changes.

Forward thinking public sector leaders want to deliver services that citizens can benefit from but they encounter off-the-shelf systems that were designed for what was needed ten years ago. Unfortunately, it is common for departments to give up on making the changes they know are needed and instead settle for carrying on with the clunky, outdated processes just because it seems easier to kick the issue down the road.

For those leaders who cannot compromise, the need to deliver new user-oriented services at all costs often comes with its own issues. They will go ahead with delivering a new digital service that works around the legacy system but this doesn't solve the problem if the legacy system they've worked around still holds critical data. The result is an ever growing list of greenfield projects and legacy applications, which become more and more difficult to manage because modernisation has done nothing to transform boring but critical internal systems.

## Skills shortages

Transforming legacy technology isn't just about systems, languages and software. A lack of relevant skills can also be a big driver of change for public sector organisations.

One side of this is upskilling technology teams in modern capabilities, so they are able to execute a transition to a cloud strategy and follow modern ways of working on an ongoing basis.

However, it is also important to recognise the urgent skills gap that many digital and technology leaders face is a shortage of people who can work with legacy technology. Even when they look outside their organisations for assistance, they may find that such skills are dying out in the wider engineering community, leaving them with little option but to work with a legacy supplier who has managed to retain a niche skill set.

A well known example of this, which is also an issue for banks and other established institutions too, is finding developers with COBOL skills, a language developed in 1959 that is still driving various core mainframe systems. If an organisation is having to rely on a handful of engineers to make changes to a core system, especially if they are contracted to a single supplier, this is a sure sign that urgent transformation is required.

# Leadership changes

Another non-technical driver of change is the urgency many thought leading public sector organisations are placing on transforming legacy technology. GDS has identified legacy IT as one of its five pillars of focus for the next decade, while the House of Commons Science and Technology Select Committee has urged GDS to conduct an audit of all government legacy systems by the end of 2020.

GDS has a clear message for all departments that the government should be cloud-first and plenty of people from within GDS have taken leadership roles at various departments over the last few years. Leadership on legacy transformation strategies isn't just coming from public sector people either. Individuals who have joined central and local government departments, agencies and public bodies from outside the sector have brought fresh ideas about building rather than buying software.

In these situations, the most important driver of legacy transformation might simply be a new person with new ideas and fresh ways of working being given the reins to drive change forward.

## Streamlining costs

Financing is such a major part of legacy transformation that it needs to be tackled separately. However, the way technology costs have changed so drastically in recent years should definitely be thought of as an important driver of change.

Cloud technologies have driven down the cost of running apps, both in terms of licensing costs and a reduction in people costs that comes from the 'shared responsibility model'. When organisations switch to this model, there's no longer a need to have staff who can physically kit out a data centre or, in the case of Platform-as-a-Service (PaaS), run an operating system. On the licensing side, open source databases such as PostgreSQL have completely eliminated the need to pay for Oracle or IBM Db2.

Key components of an organisation's infrastructure that used to be paid for upfront, like web servers and databases, can be consumed on a 'pay as you consume' basis. Therefore leaders of public sector organisations that still see money being allocated to these areas need to ask themselves why.

Modern, virtual database technology is more cost effective and generates lower overheads than legacy, on-premise data centres could ever allow. This change has been a key driver of disruption in many industries, as startups have attacked incumbents with better user experiences powered by lower technology costs. Now is the time for it to drive down the costs of legacy technology across public sector organisations.

These savings become particularly apparent when data centre costs need to be paid, including the replacement of on-premise hardware that has started to die. All of these recurring capital expenditure events should start to ring alarm bells for public sector organisations that a proper legacy transformation strategy is urgently required.

## Transformation in your organisation

Not every public sector organisation will be experiencing all of these factors at once or to the same degree. Identifying which ones are the most pressing is something all digital and technology leaders can do to assess how risky any legacy applications might be.

From there, it's a matter of money and finding a way to convince board-level executives that long-term transformation programmes are the only way to ensure your organisation doesn't become the latest victim of a legacy technology disaster.

# HOW FINANCING AFFECTS LEGACY APPLICATION TRANSFORMATION

Cost is one of the most important drivers of legacy transformation and is usually the catalyst for a much wider discussion about how to finance such projects.

From the start, it's important to realise that legacy transformation requires investment, even if it results in significantly lower running costs over the long-term. Therefore you need to develop a strong business case to back up any changes you propose.

Communicating the risks and identifying the drivers of legacy transformation are important steps for this. However, there's no getting away from the fact that you'll also need a busload of courage and commitment to convince senior colleagues that this crucial work must take place.

This might require a new approach to funding that involves lots of areas being seed funded to kick start transformation, with the aim of following up on those that can prove further investment will be worthwhile. However, this is not a one-size-fits-all solution and you should always be pragmatic and flexible about how you build support within your organisation.

## Dealing with a double hit

One of the first issues an organisation faces when developing a legacy transformation strategy is the parallel financial commitments that are required to begin with.

This occurs because transformation doesn't involve simply turning one legacy application off as you turn another modernised one on. There will be ongoing costs involved in running critical legacy applications in the short term while you create new, modernised applications. These could be significant if the cost of legacy technology was one of the main drivers of transformation in the first place.

If an organisation has decided that legacy costs are unsustainable in the long-term and that modernisation is required, it will also need to accept that this work needs upfront investment and that it must be paid for on top of any legacy running costs. Public sector leaders should be aware of this double hit from the start and be ready to prepare other senior colleagues within their organisations.

# Unavoidable upfront costs

Legacy application transformation will significantly reduce an organisation's expenditure on data centres over the long-term. However, to get to this point, there is always a capital intensive period to begin with.

Historically, funding data centres always involved a lump of capital expenditure upfront and this situation is also true of the start of a transformation project. In the case of data centre costs, the same capital expenditure will come around again and again as requirements change and hardware needs to be replaced. However, by transforming your legacy applications to be cloud-first, you can eliminate this future capital expenditure entirely and transform your financing model into "pay as you consume" expenditure.

The result is a flexible architecture that continues to renew, without the need for physical infrastructure and the capital expenditure costs that come with it. Before that though, there's still the not insignificant matter of convincing others that the upfront costs for transformation should be swallowed first.

# Convincing others to change

Without exception, it takes time for organisations to move away from legacy technology. It requires senior leaders to accept the double financial hit of maintaining critical legacy systems whilst modernising applications to the point where old technology can be decommissioned. It also means they have to be patient to see the significant benefits that these changes bring about.

Convincing senior leadership teams within public sector organisations that these programmes are worthwhile is one of the hardest parts of the transformation process. Heads of digital and technology who want to transform can take heart from the fact that tackling legacy technology is a priority for the Government, GDS and other public sector thought leaders. However, this top down direction is not necessarily enough to sway opinions within organisations.

Leaders who want to bring about change must work hard to convince others. The risks and potential impacts of not tackling legacy technologies need to be highlighted at board-level. Cyber security and the significant cost savings over the long-term need to be referenced regularly as they are likely to catch the attention of someone with the authority to give you the green light.

## The 'VC funding' model

As well as highlighting important risk factors, public sector leaders should also consider innovative funding models that might make big bills easier to swallow.

One option is to fund a number of small transformation investments, in much the same way a Venture Capital (VC) firm would invest in a lot of different startups. The reason they do this is to see which ones gain traction and are worth following up with more money. Therefore your small transformation investments should be made with clear objectives and metrics attached, in order to assess whether any progress deserves further funding.

This approach requires courage and usually relies on the assistance of a senior stakeholder who can see the long-term benefits and provide head cover for any short-term hiccups. When it pays off, this agile and incremental approach can have a truly transformative effect on major public sector organisations, as evidenced by the story of NHS Spine.

The original version of Spine, which connects patients and clinical staff to prescription services, appointment bookings and care records, was built and maintained by BT. In 2014, the NHS decided it wanted to move away from a single vendor contract that was costing it over £100m per year.

Instead of diving straight in, a proof of concept was developed[8] to demonstrate the system could be replicated using open source technology. This was then used to build a business case for the Department of Health and the Government Digital Service (GDS) in order to open up further funding and development.

By 2016, it had resulted in a new open source NHS Spine service that is run in-house. It has removed vendor lock in, allowed the team to work with small and medium-size service providers and, most significantly, saves the NHS £26 million per year and 750 working hours per day[9] on an ongoing basis.

The development of an open source proof of concept to replicate the existing BT-built service would have

---

[8]

https://www.ukauthority.com/articles/taking-nhs-spine-in-house-and-ope n-source/

[9]

https://digital.nhs.uk/news-and-events/latest-news/spine-1bn-transaction s looked like a risky project when it began. There would have been concerns that it duplicated an existing system and that the vendor might cease to co-operate if it didn't approve of the parallel work taking place.

However, the significant cost reductions and increases in maintainability demonstrate that this courageous approach has paid off in a big way.

## Mixing courage and pragmatism

Clearly, the issues around financing legacy transformation need to be tackled head on as early as possible. Failing to do so will either result in your transformation agenda never leaving the station or being derailed further down the tracks.

This process isn't simple though as some big issues need to be broached. There's the double financial hit of maintaining legacy technology while also funding transformation. There's also the fact that these early stages of transformation bring with them significant capital costs of their own.

Leaders need courage and determination to push the transformation agenda forward but they can also employ innovative approaches to finance to help convince the hard to please. This can seem daunting at first but, when you consider the huge savings that can be made from transforming legacy applications, the rewards are clearly worth the effort.

# CHAPTER 2.1

# LEGACY TRANSFORMATION IS A TEAM SPORT

When you consider the drivers of legacy transformation and the financial investment required for legacy transformation projects, it's easy to see why going it alone is not an option.

Legacy transformation is a team sport because it's hard, expensive and can take a long time, so you need to have everyone ready to push in the same direction from the start. Organisations must involve digital teams, who can deliver new applications, technology teams, who are responsible for maintaining applications, and business or service teams, who are using applications on a daily basis. The needs and frustrations of all these groups must be considered if your legacy transformation strategy is to be successful.

Building the right team from the start is also important so everyone understands how gradual changes will help to derisk the process. This can be hard when you don't have a history of working in an agile, incremental way. However, by explaining your intentions early on, you will give yourself the best chance of achieving a worthwhile transformation.

## Digital vs Technology

In many organisations, there is a divide between teams that build new user-centric applications and those who are responsible for maintaining the critical legacy systems that day-to-day services run off.

In fact, one of the reasons legacy application issues occur is that these headline grabbing new services receive investment while the boring but critical core systems are left to gradually degrade. This is never a good strategy because new applications will invariably need to interact with core legacy systems in order to be useful. Failing to engage with the people who maintain these systems will therefore only cause issues down the line.

Just as it's important to involve those who understand the art of the possible, the people who can give you a true warts and all analysis of the 'as is' state must be heard. Your IT and application support staff will be the ones who are able to add the crucial feasibility angle to any desirable idea your developers want to jump in and build.

## One team, one dream

Legacy transformation needs more than just digital and technology know-how though and every strategy must start from the same point - understanding and empathising with users.

Empathy should be the driving force behind everything the team does. This will sound familiar to many, especially those who are responsible for developing new digital services with a user-first approach. What's really important for legacy transformation is that this empathy is directed at all areas of the team, from the service or business users, to the IT maintainers and the digital developers. Each team member should understand and empathise with what drives and frustrates everyone else.

It's important to set out like this because service teams and IT maintenance teams are often overlooked in legacy application transformation. While digital teams might have an admirable urge to get on and replace legacy technology, not involving those who have been looking after these systems for 10 years or those who know how frustrating they are to use is a major mistake.

Ignoring these insights is a particularly bad idea if an organisation chooses to follow a process of iterative legacy transformation. In this scenario, the organisation might find itself in a situation where one user group is moved onto the new application, while another is left interacting with a legacy system, waiting to be moved across at a later stage. To get this right, everyone in the organisation needs to be onboard.

## Who is in the perfect team?

Building a multidisciplinary team to modernise legacy applications is important because you need to bring together people with a vision of the future and those that can actually make it happen.

Service owner - responsible for all the touchpoints involved in a public sector organisation's service, including digital and non-digital elements.

Product owner - responsible for delivering a specific digital application as part of a public sector organisation's service.

Technical architect - responsible for defining the structure of systems and applications, and how data flows between them.

Delivery manager - responsible for leading the agile and lean practices within a legacy transformation programme.

Business analyst - responsible for understanding the business needs of a service and how these fit into an organisation's strategy.

Software engineer - responsible for building and delivering any new applications, as well as making changes to existing legacy ones.

User researcher - responsible for understanding user needs and how the service might be designed to meet them.

Service designer - responsible for designing all the touchpoints involved in a public sector organisation's service, including digital and non digital elements.

Interaction designer - responsible for researching and designing the content of the service, so it helps users to complete any tasks they need to.

Support team - responsible for fixing an application when it breaks, so the service is always available for users.

Other additions - every team is different and some other people you might include are content designers, subject matter experts and performance data analysts.

As mentioned, an important driver behind building this sort of multidisciplinary team is empathising with a whole range of internal and external users from the start. Only by bringing all of these elements together at an early stage will you be able to develop a legacy transformation strategy that is desirable, feasible and viable.

## Don't forget your senior stakeholders

By building a multidisciplinary team that helps you to understand the 'as is' state and the art of possible, you are reducing the chance of unforeseen issues halting future progress.

To reduce this risk further, you should also ensure your fellow senior stakeholders are on side too. Firstly, they need to be shown why such a wide range of employees must be involved in legacy transformation. Secondly, they need to be convinced why a derisked legacy transformation strategy based on small, incremental changes makes sense in the long run.

Taking an agile approach to modernising applications involves failing fast but doing so in a way that can be rolled back quickly and easily. In this way, rapid progress can be made while derisking the sort of legacy technology disaster that others have experienced.

The issue is that senior stakeholders are used to being presented with big bang transformations, where they have a deadline to aim for, after which (they are told) all their problems will be solved. Even though history tells us these are the legacy transformations that often fail and cost huge amounts of money to fix, you need to ensure senior stakeholders understand this early on.

If not, your piecemeal strategy is in danger of getting to a stage where it looks like a mess of parallel changes being made to systems with different user groups and no end in sight. If you're not careful, your sensible and derisked agile transformation could end up appearing like you are failing to plan ahead.

Having head cover from a CEO, COO or Head of service who understands the bigger picture, and who can back you up when you're in the midst of a complex transformation programme, might be the difference between failure and success. You should therefore be engaging and educating them on the risk reduction benefits of your approach as early as possible.

## Working together from the start

Ensuring you have the right team in place to work on legacy application transformation will seem hard at first, especially if your organisation has traditionally been siloed into teams with specific, ring fenced responsibilities.

However, it might also be the most important step you take in the whole project. It will allow different areas of the organisation to see how legacy transformation can benefit them and allow you to develop a strategy that ensures it does. It will also establish a collective momentum that can help you through the inevitable hiccups that occur along the way.

Crucially though, it sets the tone for the way you will work. It establishes a foundation of empathy within the project and shows your organisation that previously overlooked areas will play a crucial role in legacy application transformation.

# MAPPING YOUR ORGANISATION DURING LEGACY APPLICATION TRANSFORMATION

Organisational mapping could go as far as identifying and interconnecting every service, system, touchpoint and individual within your organisation. This is a daunting task that isn't necessary for developing a legacy transformation strategy. However, some lightweight mapping of what people's daily routines are, how they use systems to complete tasks and why they do what they do is vital.

By this point, you will know the main drivers of legacy transformation within your organisation and these will be starting to frame the problem in your mind. This is one of the main reasons you should avoid diving into the technology straightaway and instead look at the organisation as a whole.

Rather than take your assumptions and run with them, it's important to understand how legacy applications affect the people that use them. This work will give you vital context when you dive deeper into specific applications, by allowing your team to see the real needs and frustrations of users that work with them everyday.

## Where to begin

If the prospect of mapping your organisation sounds like such a huge activity that it might stop your transformation strategy before it's even begun, do not despair. All you are aiming for is some contextual framing of how legacy applications are used, maintained and often worked around by people.

Also, it's entirely reasonable to go about mapping your organisation with an idea of why you are changing legacy applications and what any changes might look like in the future. The key thing to avoid is allowing these assumptions to restrict the questions you ask or the practices you observe.

In the first place, you want to simply engage with the people in the various service areas of your organisation and observe how they go about their daily routines.

## Empathise with the user

It's important to take a design thinking approach to mapping by focusing in the first place on building empathy for users across your organisation. One of the best ways of doing this is by 'walking the gemba', which is a key part of the lean management philosophy.

Walking the gemba involves immersing yourself in the places where the activity occurs in your organisation. It is akin to walking the shop floor in a retail environment and involves observing what really happens on a day-to-day basis, rather than what managers might report goes on. For many organisations, it will mean engaging with everything from call centres to accounts departments to help desks, in order to observe, ask questions and record what happens.

Ask the sort of questions that will uncover what really goes on, such as what are the key services a department provides? What processes are they using? What are people spending their time on? What does a regular day look like? What happens when something goes wrong? Who is the fixer? What are the blockers, frustrations and time-wasting tasks?

Try to keep your questions as open as possible and don't be afraid to ask why something is done in a certain way. This approach might reveal something unexpected but vitally important about real user behaviour.

Finally, don't forget that an important part of empathy is realising that you're probably asking some already busy people to give up their time to help you. Be respectful of people's limited time, hang out with them as they go about their regular routine and offer to help them out in return.

# Sketch the landscape

This might sound like a mammoth task but it really doesn't need to be. You are just trying to get a broad understanding of how things work and interoperate, which you can use as a jumping off point for further technical analysis and a reference resource for your team.

As you aren't trying to over analyse at this stage, it's really important to use the whole of the multidisciplinary team you've assembled to take part in this mapping exercise. You can develop a simple framework of questions to gather key insights but the most important thing is to focus on listening to people's needs and frustrations as they describe them.

This information can then be organised relatively quickly in a half day mapping workshop with your whole team. If possible, you should aim to do this as part of setting up a 'war room' for your transformation project. This is where your team will work from and the information gathered during your organisational mapping can be laid out on the walls of the room to serve as a constant visual reminder for the team.

This wallpapering doesn't need to be finished in high fidelity and can end up looking more like a police investigation room. By using post its, sharpies, string and blue tack you should be able to map out how the different areas of your organisation work together. The aim here is to review your research together and to gain a shared understanding as a team. The walls should serve as an opportunity to spark conversation and be kept up to date throughout your transformation as the team learns more.

Also, if you haven't got the space to dedicate a whole room to the project, a wall or whiteboard are good enough alternatives that provide a meeting point for stand ups and showcases.

## But, what about the tech?

For the most technical members of your team, not being able to get into the nitty gritty of the legacy applications they believe require the most transformation can be hard. It's important to be clear that this deep dive into legacy applications is just around the corner but that the user research is an important first step.

Of course, technology must be talked about in your user research too. You need to understand how systems and applications are used by people on a day-to-day basis. The distinction here is that mapping the organisation is about understanding how technology is used for good or bad and how this real user behaviour relates to the overriding aims and objectives of everyone involved.

By taking a user-centred approach to legacy transformation, which involves engaging with a broad range of internal and external user groups, you are establishing an empathetic way of working within your team. This will not only help them to understand the true value that legacy application transformation could have but also add an extra dimension to their analysis as they take a deeper dive into the technology.

# MAPPING YOUR APPLICATIONS FOR LEGACY TRANSFORMATION

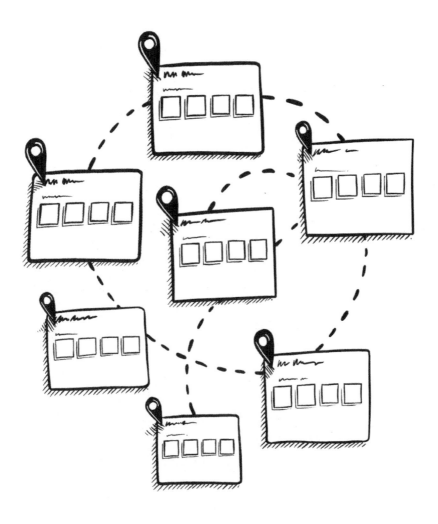

Have you ever compiled a list of every application in your organisation? If so, is it comprehensive and up-to-date?

For most organisations, the answer to both questions is usually no. While they can see why such a list would be beneficial, actually documenting this information and keeping it up to date never seems to happen. However, creating and maintaining a single source-of-truth about your application landscape is an essential part of being able to prioritise your legacy transformation work and decide on the right strategy.

To create your list, you must be analytical, data driven and should include more detail than the broad brush strokes you employed when mapping your organisation. Rather than just compiling a list of applications without much thought, you need to define a clear structure and outline the key attributes that you can compare and contrast in order to accurately account for user needs during prioritisation.

## Seeing through the fog

There is no easy or clear set of instructions you can follow to complete this task. The landscape is often unknown and requires exploration. This involves trying to identify the unknown unknowns, so that you can expect surprises and tread more carefully.

You start out on this journey with very little visibility. It's an iterative process and, with each iteration, more of the landscape becomes visible. Along the way, you'll find out about other people or teams that have knowledge to help direct you on your journey.

As no application normally stands alone, it is important to understand what dependencies applications have. There may be quick wins, such as when an application has become orphaned and can either be retired or replaced with something modern without disruption. Others might be so intertangled that extra caution and planning is required. This is where mapping the applications becomes essential, so that the right strategy is implemented to ensure any data migration happens in a safe and reliable way.

It's also worth noting that there are additional user needs to consider besides those of the end-user who interacts with the service to perform an action. For example, driving licence applications, there are the end-users who are actually applying for their licence. However, there are also the front-line staff who actually process the applications for the drivers licences, in addition to the technical team who are responsible for developing, operating and maintaining the service - each of these additional user groups should both have their needs considered too.

## What should be recorded?

It's essential to make a record of each application and its associated attributes, and also the relationships (or dependencies) that they have with one another. These will help to guide the prioritisation further on in our process.

With attributes, there are two groupings to be considered; technical and organisational. In some situations, the technical attributes are easy to identify, such as the language and version that has been used to develop it. Other examples of technical attributes might be whether it is off-the-shelf, SaaS or bespoke.

Organisational attributes often need a little more investigation and require you to find the right people to talk to. It might involve interviewing teams to answer questions like which team is responsible for supporting this application? What are the boundaries and journeys that are used? Which applications interact with it?

For each application, consider that there may be more than one instance of the application being used in the organisation. For example, a database application might be installed multiple times in an organisation for different teams and uses. Therefore instances of applications should be tracked, as each may have different priorities or require different strategies to migrate.

With so much information to record, it's important to define a schema that will be used to represent this data. This is to ensure that the data collected is done in a consistent way. With a schema in mind, you should choose which attributes to record for every application. Every attribute will not necessarily be relevant for you, so pick and choose as you see fit.

## Organisational attributes

Some ideas for organisational attributes to map for your applications are as follows:

- **Application name**
  A way to uniquely identify the application and its primary purpose that can be used to reference it as a dependency from other applications. Historically, applications may not have been named in a human friendly manner and might not be obvious.

- **Application description**
  What is the current understanding of what the application does? Why does it exist? A short "elevator-pitch" style description is all that's needed, so you could describe it to someone in the time it takes to complete a short journey in a lift.

- **Team responsibility**
  Which team is currently responsible for its operation? If further questions come out of prioritisation or when deciding on a strategy, this team will usually be able to help. It may be an IT team or an existing service team.

- **Organisational users**
  When modernisation begins, working closely with the team that interacts and uses the existing solution will help to ensure you are fulfilling user needs.

- **Application interfaces**
  How do people interact with the application? How do other applications interact with it? This can help to identify dependencies of other applications and unknown users.

- **Critical user journeys**
  What needs are being met? What needs aren't

being met? Critical user journeys are those where the organisation wouldn't be able to operate fully if one wasn't completed. When it comes to modernising, additional effort can be placed on automating the testing of these critical journeys through the application, in order to determine if a new change may break functionality.

- **Hosting**
  Where is the application hosted? This could be external, such as in the cloud, or on-premise. This may affect how you monitor (and route) traffic to and from it.

- **Retirement plan**
  Is there already a retirement or migration planned? Is there an ongoing need for its operation? Has it already been end-of-lifed? When it comes to prioritisation, based on the current lifespan plan, it may not require any modernisation effort.

- **Technical blockers**
  What known technical blockers are there? Has someone tried to modernise the application previously? What blockers have already been discovered? People might have some hidden

knowledge which may help steer priorities and strategy choice.

- **Documentation**
  Is there any documentation? This can potentially save time if it has been kept up-to-date and can be trusted. Otherwise, a full code audit may be required, which adds extra time and effort and may have an effect on prioritisation.

## Technical attributes

Technical attributes that you may want to record for your applications are:

- **Application type**
  Was this application written specifically for the organisation? Or is it a COTS or SaaS hosted solution?

- **Interface type**
  Is it a desktop based application or does it run within a browser? Is it tied to a specific browser, such as Internet Explorer? Or maybe a command line interface?

- **Programming language and version**
  Recording the programming language and version that the application was written in (if it is

bespoke and you have access to the code) will help to determine the age and risk involved with upgrading it.

- **Application framework and version**
  As with the programming language and version, if an application has been built with a particular framework, how old is that version and is there a clear and well documented upgrade path for it? For example, .NET, Ruby on Rails, Django.

- **Database and version**
  Does the application have a database behind it? If so, this can help you to assess whether the data can be easily extracted by other means, depending on the strategy.

- **Tests**
  For bespoke applications, were any automated tests or manual UAT test plans written that could be used in future if the code is refactored? Tests can also serve as documentation on how the application is meant to function.

- **Age**
  When was the application built or bought? This can be used to roughly identify technical debt that might have accrued.

- **Updates**

  When was it last updated? Six years or six days ago? Both can help to identify what activity the application has seen and help to determine whether documentation is worth seeking. They can also indicate the potential scale of technical debt accrued.

- **Mean time to repair (MTTR)**

  On average (and if known), how long does it take to repair an issue and have it deployed? For applications that have a fast MTTR, it may mean a process is well documented which can aid any potential modernisation.

- **Issue volume**

  Record the average number of issues that are raised for the application every month. If an application has a consistently high volume of issues, that could mean it has a high cost to support and maintain in its current state.

## Where should this information be recorded?

You should treat this exercise as a data-driven analysis and therefore record this information in a way that lets you easily extract, query and calculate various factors from it. This will allow you to score different applications and prioritise transformation.

Ensure that when you record the information about an application, and its attributes and dependencies, that these are stored individually, so that they can be moved around on lists, however you are storing this data; whether physically on cards, a whiteboard, or on an online system. There are many iterations to mapping and prioritisation yet to come, so being able to juggle the order of these application records around is essential.

You want the data that will drive those decisions to be in a single source of truth, which is easy to amend and can evolve as more data is discovered. The data should also be visible to all those who need it. A central spreadsheet can work well or even a non-technical solution such as a whiteboard or post-it notes with string to show dependencies. The key takeaway is that it needs to be the single source of truth.

## How to find the information

You will already have a high-level overview of the organisational landscape from the mapping you've done. The objective here is to investigate and dig deeper into the various applications.

Invite teams or individuals to workshops if you believe they may have knowledge of specific applications. A good idea would be to run a whiteboard workshop where everyone can see the same mapping and point things out as a group. Ensure that you encourage everyone to share even the smallest detail that might be related. They might think it's irrelevant but that small thing could become quite important the further you dig. Also, build out a picture of who isn't present but might have further information and repeat the process with them.

Try to seek out hidden treasures within your organisation. Someone, somewhere, at sometime may have already tried to collect and collate the information you are looking for. There might be a spreadsheet hidden away on an email thread or folder on someone's computer that could be a goldmine of documentation or listings that you need.

If it's possible to view the source code of applications, that's always an option too. Roll up your sleeves and dive in. You'll hopefully be able to piece together some of the logic to understand application boundaries, expecting inputs and outputs, and which systems talk to one another.

# Build your single source-of-truth

As mentioned, this will be an iterative process and you may use multiple methods to collect this data. Act like an investigative journalist and keep seeking out answers by following up with questions to build an understanding of your application ecosystem that complements your organisational mapping.

Remember that what you are aiming for is a single source of truth, visible to everyone in your transformation team and anyone else in the wider organisation that needs to see it. It will be essential for the next stage of prioritisation but can also serve as a living record that helps to reduce technical debt and your reliance on legacy technology for years to come.

# PRIORITISING YOUR
# APPLICATION TRANSFORMATION

After you have mapped your application ecosystem as best as you can, you should begin work on prioritising which applications to modernise first.

Lots of variables can help you to determine a priority order but it's important to remember that it's not rocket science. It's mostly just a common sense approach to evaluating and balancing the various factors and needs of your organisation.

Security and maintainability are important reasons to modernise legacy applications. If software ages and is not maintained, then security vulnerabilities can be discovered over time and it can become difficult to roll out the required upgrades to plug these holes. Security and maintainability come hand in hand.

It's also important to consider budget constraints. These may result in you choosing a particular transformation approach for an application or in deciding to modernise a different application altogether. In making these choices, you will need to weigh up the business value of transforming an application against the technical effort required to do so.

# What affects prioritisation?

Some modernisation tasks may take longer than others or take longer than expected, so you might find yourself needing to juggle conflicting priorities. You may also find that a new piece of information surfaces when you are following up on your application mapping that has a knock on effect on your priority order.

While it's important to be aware that these issues might crop, you can get on with prioritisation by weighing up technical effort and business value.

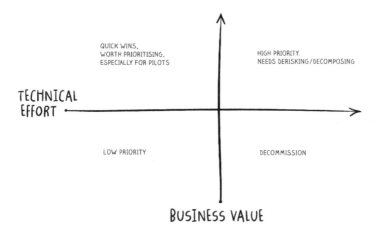

The diagram above serves as a simple guide to how these factors might steer your decision. Using the attributes you have collected during your application mapping, you can identify the technical effort an application may require and the business value it represents.

As mentioned, the security and maintainability of an application are key considerations when prioritising. However, you might also have an urgent need to alter an application's behaviour to add a new or adapt an existing feature based on changing user needs. If it is difficult or impossible to add or change the functionality of an application in its current state, the business value of the feature change may be significant enough for the organisation to trump all other considerations.

## Review priorities regularly

Just as you needed to create a single source-of-truth when mapping your applications, you need to create a single list of applications to track your transformation priorities. This should be reviewed on a regular basis because priorities can change if, as mentioned, new information is gathered.

Set a recurring review session in the calendar and remember that if no change in prioritisation has occurred, it's not a waste of a review meeting - it just confirms that your current order is still correct.

If priorities do change, it's not anyone's fault either. You should just accept that a change in priorities has occurred, that you've caught it early on and that you can therefore pivot.

## What are you trying to achieve?

Without a priority order list, you'd be taking a gamble on which application to modernise first.

What you actually want is a list of prioritised scores for each application, based on the attributes from the mapping work you've already done. This scorecard will help you to make an informed decision about which applications to work on first. The quadrant diagram above, paired with your mapping information, will allow you to rank applications into your prioritised list.

You may need to do a few iterations of your priority list before deciding on an initial order because a priority for one application might affect another. Upcoming deadlines is one example of how applications may affect the priority of others, potentially around support contracts or licence renewals. Until you have done one iteration of all applications, you won't be able to compare those deadlines against one another. However, this will be possible in a second iteration.

This is why reviewing the priority list at regular intervals is important. You can check what progress is being made and, if slower than initially estimated, revise your priorities to account for changes. By doing this, you'll ensure you are not left needing to renew a costly licence or contract for one application because the transformation of another took up all your time.

## Gather different viewpoints

It is important to consider the people in your organisation that might use or be involved with the application.

For example, the product manager and the service owner might see different parts of the picture within the organisation. Similarly, if different departments are involved in the support and running of an existing application, they might have different needs to factor in.

## Technical factors

When considering the technical effort required to modernise an application, some questions worth asking are:

- **How up-to-date is the application?**
  If it is a bespoke application, you need to consider the versions of the programming language and application framework that it has been written in. How many versions behind the most recently released one is the application? What are the known security vulnerabilities of the version that your application is currently using? The difference between versions will steer the technical effort required, as upgrade paths are not always clear or simple. Plus, frameworks and other third-party dependencies might not just be drop-in replacements.

  If it is a Commercial Off The Shelf (COTS) application, how many versions behind the most recently released one are you? Is there an automated or clear upgrade path you can follow? Will an upgrade break any integrations that expect functionality or data to be available in a particular format or structure?

- **How complex is the application?**
  For bespoke applications where you have source code to maintain, is it written with hundreds of lines of code or hundreds of thousands of lines of code? Each line of code increases the complexity of maintenance and

the burden on ensuring that functionality does
not break.

- **How well tested is the application?**
  With the application complexity comes the
  question of what sort of automated tests are
  there for the code? If tests exist that can check
  if functionality works as expected, you can use
  those as a safety net to ensure it works as
  expected when upgrades need to happen. In
  this way, you can ensure other applications or
  users that interact with it won't have any
  surprises.

- **When was the application last released?**
  If an application hasn't been released in a while,
  there is the risk that instructions or even
  automated pipelines to deployment might be
  out-of-date or broken. This might be a hurdle
  that blocks you from putting a modernised
  application in front of users.

## Business/organisation factors

When considering the business value of modernising
an application, some questions worth asking are:

- **How much are licences costing you?**
  For COTS, how much do the licences cost for the application? Would it be worth saving the money for this license by replacing COTS with a bespoke application? Also, is there a renewal deadline? Would you like to save money by having the application replaced or decommissioned before that date?

- **What support contracts exist?**
  Depending on how COTS or bespoke applications are hosted, do you have to pay large support contracts that are squeezing budgets? If you want new functionality or to change existing functionality, do you have to pay large fees?

- **Does the COTS feature roadmap align with organisation?**
  Before making the decision to remain with a COTS application, does the future of that application match the predicted needs of your organisation? Might the company that develops the software take a radical new direction with the application? If so, have you considered that you might be stuck with the version you have or be forced onto a bespoke system later?

## Considering interdependencies

It's important to consider interdependencies between applications while you are prioritising. What you want to avoid is duplicated or wasted effort when modernising applications that affect others.

If an application depends on another directly, or further down a chain of dependencies, do you need to consider which order you modernise those applications? If you modernise one of the applications, does that mean you'll then need to alter the way that application communicates with another?

You wouldn't want to finish modernising one application and then start with others, to find these subsequent applications have changed in such a way that you need to revisit the first one to ensure it continues to communicate.

Develop a few iterations of your priority list using the application mapping work you've done to identify interdependencies and work out the order for prioritising these dependency chains. After all, the destiny of one application's modernisation may be tightly coupled to another.

## Choosing your top priority

If we look back to our quadrant diagram:

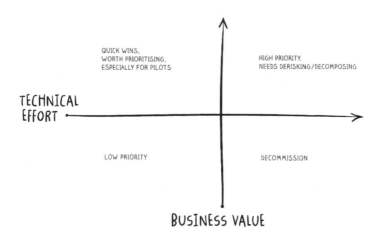

A workshop would be an ideal format to iterate through your list of applications a few times to work out your first priorities. The iterations of the list can be based on the factors we have discussed so far and listed below. After each iteration, the priority may change and should be reordered accordingly:

1.  Business value
2.  Technical effort
3.  Upcoming deadlines
4.  Interdependencies

With the two axes in our quadrant diagram, technical effort and business value, you'll need to ensure that you invite the correct people to give an opinion on each from their different perspectives.

Some example prioritisation scenarios may be:

- A number of applications that have a number of dependency upgrades available that contain security fixes. So long as they pass automated tests highlighting that the upgrades will not break functionality—as this would increase the technical effort required—these could be updated rapidly with the benefit of increased security over a wide area of applications. These would be low technical effort but mid-high business value.

- An application that has an expensive support contract renewal looming but is not easy to change to meet new user needs. If a bespoke solution could be created to replace it, that would mean this application becomes a low business value item and could be decommissioned, so that the costly renewal costs can be avoided.

- A legacy bespoke application that is of high/critical business value, though also high technical effort to modernise. The risks of not being able to fix security vulnerabilities and make changes to meet user needs means this should be a top priority, as the risk to the organisation is too high if it were to fail.

- Applications that don't pose a significant risk to an organisation due to low business value and low technical effort that can be dealt with at a later time once the higher risk items are handled.

After the prioritisation workshop, you may have a clear priority list that allows you to decide on the best transformation strategy for the top application, before working your way through the other applications. If the top positions in your list are still hard to determine though, things may become clearer as you consider the transformation strategies for each application.

Either way, let's continue by looking at the various transformation strategies you could employ in the next section.

# DECIDING ON THE RIGHT LEGACY TRANSFORMATION STRATEGY

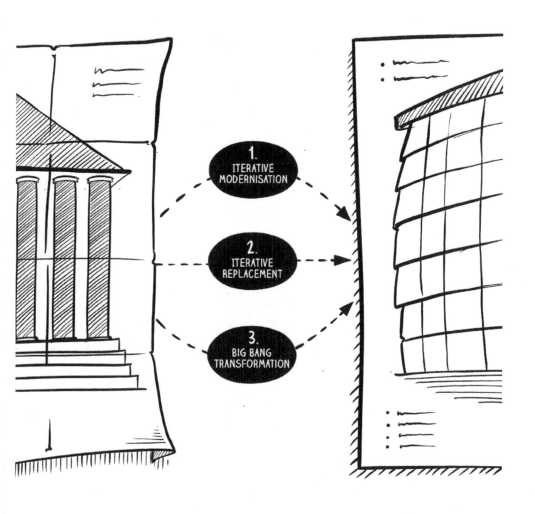

Having mapped your applications and chosen which applications to prioritise, the next major milestone in your journey is deciding which transformation strategy to employ.

Up to now, you've worked out why you need to transform your legacy applications, what their current states are and which need to be changed as soon as possible. In doing so, you've uncovered a wealth of useful information and newly discovered visibility about your organisation's technology landscape.

Now you are in the ideal position to choose how you go about ensuring your applications become supportable, maintainable and, crucially, designed around user needs.

## Understanding your options

In this chapter, we introduce each strategy and then cover them in greater detail in subsequent chapters. You should try to understand all the strategies before deciding which is the right one for each legacy application you want to transform.

The factors you will need to consider when making this decision are wide-ranging. They include technical considerations, such as whether you can access an application's source code, resourcing issues, such as whether a development team has the capacity to deliver a particular strategy, and your appetite for risk.

It's also important to realise that you won't necessarily be able to identify the right strategy straight away. You might start with one strategy and then, as you discover more about an application, need to pivot and alter it.

This isn't a problem, especially if you follow an iterative process. What's important is that you understand what each strategy entails and then use the information you have gathered so far about your applications, as well as any new information you discover, to pick the right one.

## Will iterative modernisation work for you?

Iterative modernisation is where you take an existing application's codebase and selectively tackle parts of it piece by piece to update it into a more secure and maintainable state.

Breaking down the modernisation tasks into smaller chunks reduces the risk of transformation, as you can more easily test the changes you're making. It also makes it easier to reverse those changes if something goes wrong.

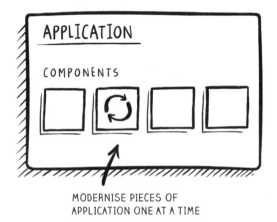

MODERNISE PIECES OF
APPLICATION ONE AT A TIME

If you have an existing bespoke application and can perform a quick code audit, you might determine that iterative modernisation is technically feasible. A code audit could include the following checks:

- You have access to the source code
- You can compile the application without errors (if it requires compilation)
- You can run the application in its current state
- You can confirm that any third-party dependencies it uses are still available

If one or more of the above are not feasible immediately, you should investigate what effort would be required to make them possible. In doing so, you should limit the time you spend on these investigations, so you don't spend too long on a fruitless search.

You might choose iterative modernisation if you can give the application a fresh lease of life by introducing modern software practices, such as continuous integration and delivery (CI/CD) pipelines, and automated testing. This can result in security updates and releases becoming painless, as well as new features designed around changing user needs being made and released in a reasonable time frame.

If you are considering iterative modernisation, it's vital to ensure there is a team available to take on the responsibility of maintaining and securing the application over its lifetime. Without giving a team that ownership and responsibility, the application could easily fall back into a legacy state if it is not maintained once modernised. This team needs to be comfortable working with the technologies the application was originally written in and be able to implement modern software practices in those technologies too.

# Should you iteratively replace your application?

For legacy off-the-shelf applications, or ones with an extremely large code footprint that are not in a good enough condition to modernise, you should consider the merits of an iterative replacement strategy.

It involves replacing parts of the application with newly written code or, alternatively, introducing new applications that replace some of the functions of the legacy application. You replace these parts iteratively, rather than in one go, so that risk is reduced.

ITERATIVE REPLACEMENT

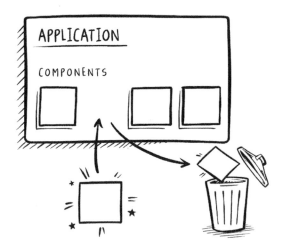

When you are iteratively replacing a legacy application with a new bespoke application, you must consider whether you have a team available to do the development work. There must also be a team available to perform ongoing support and maintenance afterwards.

An alternative to replacing with a new bespoke application is using a SaaS (software-as-a-service) or off-the-shelf application to replace parts of your legacy application. When considering software that you don't develop or maintain yourself, it's important to choose products that embrace modern standards towards APIs and data handling, which do not sell or misuse public data. By doing so, you'll allow yourself to get out of contracts in the future and take back your data without requiring another major transformation.

## Is big-bang transformation your only option?

If you're unable to iteratively modernise or replace an application, you're left with the option of replacing the entire application and all its components in one "big-bang" release.

The big-bang strategy gets its name from the scientific theory; just like the universe, a new application comes into existence all at once. There is no journey of small iterations before launch, just a big BANG.

Explosions are dangerous and the same is true of this transformation strategy, as the aftermath of a release going wrong makes it inherently riskier than the iterative approaches we have already discussed. However, a big-bang strategy is sometimes necessary and, if it is, you need to look for ways to de-risk it.

BIG-BANG TRANSFORMATION

One of the main things to consider is data. Firstly, you need to assess how accessible the data in your existing application is. Then, you should work out if you can export the data in a file format that can be imported into a new application.

If this is possible, one option worth exploring is whether you run a replacement application with the imported data in parallel with the existing application. As long as you can keep the data in sync, your users can use both applications at the same time and you can revert to the original application if the new one doesn't work as expected when you switchover.

Of course, running two systems in parallel may not be feasible. Data access or licensing costs may mean you can only have one system running at a time. In these cases you should try to "dry-run" the rollout of the new application. This might involve creating a test environment where you replicate what the live application is and practice the big-bang release there, without using real world data.

As you might have realised, there is often a big investment involved in doing a big-bang release. Being an inherently risky approach, you will incur costs from having to take extra precautions. For example, what will you do if everything goes wrong? Do you have teams in place that are ready to deal with the fallout?

Plus, you'll still have to ensure that the new application is maintainable and supportable, so that you are not just creating tomorrow's legacy today.

## How to decide which strategy to employ

It's a good idea to evaluate the strategies sequentially, starting with iterative modernisation, then iterative replacement and finally a big-bang transformation.

You should consider iterative modernisation first because, if your application is bespoke and can be modernised, it might well be the quickest and most cost effective approach. If modernisation isn't possible, you can start to consider iterative replacement. Try to keep a big-bang transformation as an option of last resort, as it is the most risky.

You may find that more than one approach is feasible. If they are, you can start to weigh up the other pros and cons for each one, such as the time and costs involved.

You should also consider your organisation's goals and objectives, such as whether it wants to become more technically self-sufficient in future. If this is the case, then you may prefer a strategy that gives you the opportunity to modernise an application or develop a replacement, rather than using something off-the-shelf.

## Iterate, reevaluate and pivot

You won't necessarily be able to identify the right strategy straight away. Each strategy is explained in more detail in subsequent chapters so make sure you are fully aware of what they entail before making your decision.

Also, don't be afraid to make a decision because you believe you won't be able to turn back from it. By following an iterative process, you can start with one strategy and then pivot and alter it without this causing a major issue.

What's really important to remember is that you should choose the right individual strategy for each individual application. If you're planning to transform more than one, don't just pick one strategy for all of them. By understanding the detail behind each strategy, you'll be able to pick the right one at the right time for each legacy application you want to transform.

# ITERATIVE MODERNISATION
# OF LEGACY APPLICATIONS

This strategy is all about reviving an existing application from the murky depths of legacy and giving it a fresh lease of life so it's maintainable and sustainable. Doing so in an iterative way will reduce the risks involved because you'll be able to test improvements more easily, as they take place in smaller iterations of work.

If you decide to use this strategy, there are many best practices you can apply to further the support and maintenance of an existing application. It's really a matter of deciding how far you want to go, as well as how much time and money you want to invest.

ITERATIVE MODERNISATION

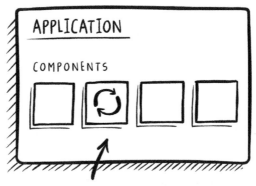

MODERNISE PIECES OF
APPLICATION ONE AT A TIME

# When to choose iterative modernisation

Your rationale for wanting to get your application into a maintainable and sustainable state will be driven by a desire to then be able to evolve it in future. During your research and planning you will have seen signs that there is still value in the application for it to be invested in rather than retired.

However, to choose this strategy, you need certain things to be in place and certain things to be possible. You need to be able to see a future path that involves continuing the investment in and evolution of the technology beyond the initial modernisation stage. In the case of off-the-shelf software, you may simply want to get your application into a state from where you can upgrade the product.

You will also need to consider whether you have the right capabilities at your disposal and the right access to the codebase to make iterative modernisation possible.

## A supportable technology stack

You need to consider if the application and its current technology stack is one that you can maintain going forward. The stack will likely include any software languages, frameworks and dependencies, and any dependent systems or services it requires to run.

When you consider all these elements, can you see an upgrade path for the technology stack in the future? Security vulnerabilities can be discovered at any moment in any part of an application and, if the maintainers of that component are no longer releasing security updates, it might be risky to retain the existing stack. Even if you can see a path that would be possible, you should consider how expensive and resource heavy it would be before deciding iterative modernisation is the right choice.

## A capable development team

There are also wider considerations about whether you can allocate a team to be responsible for the application and whether they are capable of developing the application with the existing technology stack.

Your first consideration should be about the team you have available right now. Does it have the capabilities to modernise the application itself? Furthermore, would it be able to maintain it going forward so it doesn't become legacy once again? You may decide it can do both but would require some investment to do so, and therefore you need to decide whether that investment is possible.

If you decide that your existing team doesn't have the right capabilities or that specific investment in the team isn't possible, you might still choose iterative modernisation by outsourcing the work to a supplier. Again, you need to decide what money is available to do this and whether time or budget restrictions make outsourcing a better option than in-housing.

## Access to a manageable codebase

To iteratively modernise an application, you will first need to access the codebase and weigh up whether its scale and complexity make this strategy a viable option.

If you can't find the code straightaway, can you figure out how to access it relatively easily? With access to the source code, you should start by checking whether it can be compiled, if it requires compilation. If it fails to compile, is there enough debug information to help you resolve any issues?

You should also consider the complexity and scale of the codebase. Is it a couple of hundred lines long or hundreds of thousands of lines? If you are dealing with a small application that will take you a long time to modernise, it might be easier to just replace it.

It may take some time to dig around in the code and fully understand if iterative modernisation is possible. You may find it is so complex that you need to adjust your strategy but this shouldn't be seen as a problem. Rather, it is a stage in the iterative process, which will teach you a lot about the application as you move forward.

# Steps to take, decisions to make

When you proceed with an iterative modernisation, you are aiming to get your application into a maintainable, sustainable state that your team is then able to evolve in the future. It should become easy to upgrade with security patches and provide a foundation from which you can plot a path for future investment in the technology.

## Set your goals

Your first aim is to improve the application so that it is at least maintainable and supportable. In doing so, you might choose to decommission parts of it that are redundant while investing in other areas of the codebase that you consider to be valuable.

Just making an application maintainable and supportable might not be enough for your organisation though and you may need to change or add new functionality that enables you to meet an organisational or user need. Setting this sort of goal may also help you to access the budget for modernisation, as it may prove to your organisation that the investment is worthwhile because the application will be adding new value.

You may also decide that, once you have reached the point of maintainability and sustainability, you will consistently invest in this technology for a given number of years. In this way, you have set an immediate modernisation goal and a further aspirational that justifies the modernisation phase.

## Start with an audit

Once you've decided where you need to get to, you should start auditing the application to assess how you can get to this desired state. In doing so, you want to build your understanding of how it is architected and should draw on your earlier application mapping to help you start digging around.

Run the application on a development machine, boot it up and run some tests on it. Ask yourself some questions about how it behaves. Is there an automated test suite and/or a manual test plan you can try out? Do you know how to deploy it? Do you fully understand its dependencies and whether they are up to date? If it's bespoke software, is the code easy to understand and follow?

What you are trying to do is understand where the value exists in the code and which the riskiest bits of it are. You may find that code analysers help you to identify where a lot of complex business logic exists. What you need to do is try to understand the value of this logic, so you can decide whether it can be picked up and run elsewhere or be modernised bit by bit.

If tests are in place, they will help you to understand how the application works, whether from a user perspective or at a code-level, and will tell you if the application is behaving as expected.

## Implement a test harness

Tests that are already in place will help you to check nothing breaks when you start to refactor code or upgrade versions and dependencies. But what should you do if tests do not touch large parts of the code or do not exist at all?

In this situation, you can write new automated ones that test the application from a user perspective, and, if you are modernising bespoke software, from a code perspective too. These are collectively known as a test harness.

It will help you to describe and verify how the application works before you start making any changes. Essentially, using a test harness is reverse engineering test driven development (TDD), so you write some rules to assert whether the code behaves as you expect when you provide it with inputs. If the tests pass, you will have a pretty good idea that you won't break anything when you make changes.

## Replatform the application

If moving to the cloud is a key driver for modernising your application, you need to get it running on a new platform. While doing so, you should ensure that deployment and monitoring are automated.

You want to automate deploys so they are no longer done via a manual process that is slow and susceptible to error. Then you want to ensure that you have tests in place to show whether an application is live and working. You can make further use of your test harness by running this suite of tests against your live environment. It is then acting as a series of high level monitors to check whether all the regular processes you expect the application to perform are not broken.

## Refactor the application

With your test harness in place, you can now safely upgrade dependencies and run your test suite to assert it still works as expected. It is advisable to make changes to dependencies that are as small as possible, perhaps one by one, so you can quickly detect which change is causing your test suite to fail.

For bespoke software, you can then start to improve the code by refactoring it. The automation you have started to introduce by this stage should give you confidence to make changes to the code. You can make a change and have the tests run at a click of a button, so you've established a continuous integration continuous deployment (CI CD) pipeline.

You may want to consider making your application 12 factor compliant[10] too, so that it adheres to practices that make it more maintainable and, crucially for replatforming, more portable. We've also written a productionisation checklist[11] that you can use as a

---

[10] https://12factor.net/
[11] https://productionisation.io/

guide to the minimum standards required for maintainable software.

## Add new value

At this point your team should be able to add new functionality to the application if desired and needed. As they add, change or remove functionality they should actively maintain the test harness and evolve it at the same time as making changes, much like the TDD approach of red, green, refactor.

Remember that you set out to get your application into a maintainable and sustainable state that provides a baseline from which you can add functionality. By now you should have a plan for continuing to invest in the application going forward. It's time to celebrate with your team.

# Issues you may encounter

As you take the steps outlined above, you may encounter a range of issues. These will depend on the particular circumstances of the application you are attempting to modernise and the team responsible for doing the work.

Some of these issues may only become obvious when you first get to grips with the code, such as how difficult it is to untangle and extract any business logic from it. You may also encounter issues as you discover more about the tests that are in place, how much work is required to improve them and whether entirely new ones are needed.

## Complexity of business logic

How complex is the code or configuration that represents the business logic of the application?

If it's spaghetti code - a mess of many lines of code that are hard for anyone to understand and follow - it'll be hard to untangle and get to a stage where it is easy enough to understand and extract the core business logic from. Configuration and settings can be just as messy too.

This is where tests and a test harness can be used to understand how the application behaves and what value can be retained. You should use this approach to make minor changes at a time, moving cautiously as you gradually build up your understanding.

## Bugs and workarounds

Within spaghetti code, there will potentially be bugs. The people who use the application may have adapted and developed workarounds for these known bugs. Working around them has become second nature, to the point where people don't even need to think about them or consider them as bugs anymore. What you need to consider is that the bug's behaviour is now expected behaviour.

When modernising, do you fix these bugs, potentially breaking the workarounds people have developed over the years? Or leave them in place to retain the existing behaviour that people expect? Do you have a clear picture of who and what is using the application, in order to be able to make this decision?

First of all, you should seek out documentation to determine why something has been implemented in the way it has. Most importantly though, you need to focus on user needs at this point. You must bring users along with any changes you make or plan to make through regular showcases and training. In this way, you can change behaviours as you fix bugs.

### Discontinued software dependencies

When you do go to upgrade certain dependencies for the application, you may find that they are not available. Alternatively, you may find that they run on old technology or software run on old technology that doesn't match your modernisation strategy.

You need to consider whether you can replace the dependency wholesale. For example, if you're dealing with a database dependency, could you move the schema?

At some point during these considerations, cost will start to outweigh the benefits. You may feel that the extra cost is worthwhile in order to make your modernisation possible or this issue may be one of the reasons you start to consider iterative replacement instead.

# If iterative modernisation won't work

It may turn out that the existing codebase or technology stack becomes a hurdle that your team is unable to overcome. You may also attempt iterative modernisation but discover obstacles that halt your progress with this strategy.

Any development that you have done up to this point won't have been wasted though and you may be able to pivot towards an iterative replacement strategy instead. In doing so, you can use any knowledge you have built up about the application's components to work out whether it's possible to replace them rather than modernise the existing code.

# ITERATIVE REPLACEMENT OF LEGACY APPLICATIONS

If you decide that iterative modernisation of your application is not possible, you should consider whether following an iterative replacement strategy might work. At first, you may feel some disappointment at not being able to modernise an application, if people use it everyday and it is achieving certain user needs.

However, if getting the application into a state where making security, maintenance or user-focused changes is impossible through modernisation, it's time to weigh up the merits of replacement. Just as with iterative modernisation, it involves breaking the application down into workable components. What's different is that you then use newly developed or off-the-shelf software to replace them.

ITERATIVE REPLACEMENT

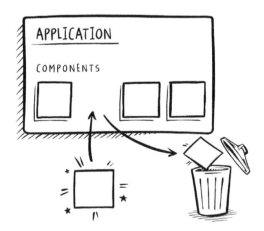

# When to choose iterative replacement

You can turn to iterative replacement if you realise modernisation won't be possible but there are other factors that will help you decide whether it is a viable approach for what you are attempting.

## A vital application for your organisation

You should consider this approach if the application you're trying to modernise is a vital organisational cog that certain critical processes rely on. It may be the case that a team has already tried to modernise the application but found that the code was too much of a mess to work with or that the technology stack was impossible to revive.

As your business processes are tied to this application, you may also be reluctant to buy or build new software to replace it as this might mean having to change your processes too. Overall, this may be very expensive when you consider all the costs associated with replacing software, migrating data and training people. To reduce the impact of this disruption, you can replace your legacy application iteratively with a new one that better meets your organisational needs over time.

If you're replacing off-the-shelf software, your only modernisation option may be to upgrade to a new version. This could involve paying for a more expensive upgrade licence and potentially having to change existing processes, if the new version is quite different to the old. In this case, you might choose to build new software that replaces each piece of functionality one piece at a time or iteratively move to smaller off-the-shelf replacements that are a better fit for your organisation's needs or use a combination of both.

## User needs outweigh development costs

Delivering value to your organisation and its users by meeting user needs is of paramount importance and if this can be best achieved by delivering bespoke software or an off-the shelf replacement, it's likely worth the cost and can be justified.

When weighing up an iterative replacement strategy you need to calculate the cost of building custom applications, any new off-the-shelf applications and any dependencies you need to iteratively replace. On the other hand, you should consider the relative cost of being tied to a legacy software vendor and its off-the-shelf software, especially if its roadmap does not align with yours and it doesn't add the features you need.

Ultimately, this choice comes down to organisational mindset. Is the legacy application you are assessing both user-focused and well-aligned with your needs? If so, costs are normally swallowed. If not, you will always be needing to adapt user behaviour to the software at hand. The software should work for the user, rather than the user working for the software, and you should choose a replacement that fulfils this brief.

Replacing software will always require some element of business process change too. However, by working in small iterations, you can test how the changes work for all users and reduce the risk throughout.

# Steps to take, decisions to make

You can choose to iteratively replace with bespoke or off-the-shelf software. Whichever you choose, you need to ensure that the software fills the legacy void and works with the other components in the application you are modernising. If you don't, you might break the interfaces that other components depend on.

When iteratively replacing an application, you should stick to the Government Digital Service (GDS) principles of understanding user needs and delivering in an agile way that iteratively progresses through discovery, alpha, beta and live phases. Essentially, you will be replacing bits of your application and moving users from one system to another with this approach, so keeping the user needs front of mind throughout is crucial.

## Defining components to be replaced

In order to iteratively replace the components of an application, you need to work out how to "decompose" the application. How do you define the different components that you will replace? For each component, if you can't find an off-the-shelf replacement, then you'll need to use a bespoke build of a new component. Are the user needs being met for each component you replace?

Rather than break an application down into components that are taken directly from the structure of the code, consider breaking it down into the functionality of how it addresses user needs. Then you can look for solutions that do that thing well and find potential off-the-shelf software options.

For example, if your existing application has case management and document management built into one, you might be able to find a solution that does document management really well. It could be used to replace this specific task, rather than trying to find a product that does document management as well as case management.

By trying to reduce the surface area of the application you're working on, you can slice up the functionality into components to be replaced.

## Assessing off-the-shelf replacements

If you do consider any off-the-shelf software, look at the product roadmaps. What does the future hold for this product?

It may take time and effort to introduce this replacement into your organisation so you need to ensure the investment is worthwhile. Check that planned features align with your users' needs, as you will be beholden to what the developers of the software choose to implement. Get it wrong and you could find yourself needing to replace this component once again in the near future.

Finally, you must avoid outsourcing the procurement of any replacements to another department that hasn't been involved in understanding the user research you've done. If you don't, all the hard work you've done to ensure your legacy transformation is driven by meeting user needs could be undone by people who think other factors are more important.

## Reflecting user needs in your architecture

Once you have defined components and assessed replacements, you need to come back to the architecture of your application and, once again, overlay your users' needs in order to decide what the future state of the application should look like.

This is because you must assess how changing different components will affect all connected user workflows. For example, if you are replacing parts of an ERP system that has accounting, invoicing, payroll and CRM components, you could move one of them but they may all rely on data from each other. You might find that breaking them is not possible and that your replacement processes need to be brought together.

User needs will dictate the stages of change, so your technical approach to replacing components needs to mirror this and determine the sequencing of changes you make.

## Slice and sequence the problem

As you replace components, the changes should be sliced into small chunks that balance disruption and cost, while also considering the sequencing from a user perspective.

The changes you make to replace certain workflows will involve moving users and onboarding them onto new systems. This will involve running two systems in parallel for some time and you don't want this to just drag on and on for too long. Therefore you need to balance the risk of moving users with the disruption caused by having parallel systems.

As mentioned, you will want to reflect user needs in the architecture and may choose to make bigger replacements in one go, so as to not disrupt users too much for too long. Of course, this increases the risk if something goes wrong, so you will need to decide on your appetite for risk and disruption.

Finally, your sequencing may also be decided by the resources you have available. If there's one team to work on the application, this may dictate whether you think of replacing one component at a time whereas, if there are two teams, you could replace two at a time.

## Retire legacy components

Once your replacements are live and you have moved users, you will gradually come to realise that legacy parts of the application are still live but with few or no users using them. This is a milestone to celebrate but also a point at which you need to consider how you fully retire these components.

While you should take your time to ensure that these parts of the old application really aren't being used, this will essentially come down to turning servers off and seeing whether anyone complains. Of course, you should also have tests in place to automatically check that nothing essential has been broken.

If something does break or someone does complain, your planning has hopefully ensured that it isn't too much of a problem and you can see this issue as an as yet undiscovered need to be addressed in a future feature.

# Issues you may encounter

It's important to remember that the end result of iterative replacement is the same as with a big bang transformation - the legacy application will be replaced by a new one. By adopting an iterative approach though, you are reducing risk by replacing functionality gradually and providing some level of functionality for users on an ongoing basis.

## Switchovers may go wrong

One of the big risks of iterative replacement comes when you switch out old components for new ones. When you do, you need to be ready for two outcomes. It could go well, in which case you proceed to test and move on.

If a switchover goes badly though, you may need to revert while preserving the integrity of any data. You may not be able to run the old and new at the same time because your data may be polluted, either with duplication or synchronisation issues between the two. To avoid these issues, you should develop a "go live checklist", which defines rollback procedures in case anything goes wrong.

## Overcoming complexity takes time

In attempting to mitigate these risks and take caution over data handling, your iterative replacement may take a lot longer than it would to replace everything all at once.

Access to the underlying data is essential for iterative replacement. If you need to read and write from a database, your new replacement needs to be able to read and write from that same central store, as do the legacy components of the application. This can be complex and require a lot of thought to enable both systems to work side-by-side.

Also, when you're rewriting parts of the application, you may change behaviour within other parts. It might be that you find a bug in the old application and fix it with the replacement. If you do, you need to consider the knock-on effects of your change and determine whether any applications are working on the basis that a bug's behaviour still occurs.

## Getting lost in the detail

As you are iterating through replacing various workflows, you might feel like the process is becoming a bit of a mess, with systems running in parallel, different users at different stages of onboarding and service, IT and operations teams straddling all of it.

Using weekly sprints to iterate and improve quickly and steadily is the right approach but it's also important to keep the bigger picture in mind. Otherwise, it can feel like a bit of a pressure cooker that's ready to pop with no end in sight for the project. To ensure you don't get stuck in the weeds of each workflow, take a step back every couple of months to reflect, revise and replan.

# When iterative transformation isn't possible

If you started off hoping that you'd be able to iteratively replace or modernise your legacy application but have realised it won't be possible, it might feel like a failure to have to resort to a big-bang transformation. This isn't true.

While it's certainly the case that many people dismiss this sort of approach as dated and debunked, the reality is that technical and organisational factors can sometimes make it impossible to choose anything else. If this is the case for you, what is most important is that you do it in a way that allows you to derisk your big-bang transformation.

# CHAPTER 3.4

## HOW TO MAKE A SUCCESS OF A BIG BANG TRANSFORMATION

If an iterative and incremental approach to transformation isn't possible, you are left with the option of transforming your application in one big-bang release.

This inherently risky approach, which involves replacing the entire application and all its components in one go, should only be attempted as a last resort. In a world where agile is often the preferred software development approach, even discussing the idea of a big-bang transformation can seem like bringing up the elephant in the room.

These conversations must take place though as it's sometimes the only sensible or feasible choice. Agile transformations that involve incremental and iterative change simply aren't suited to some complex applications. However, this doesn't mean there aren't lessons from agile that can't be applied to a big bang approach.

In fact, by embracing some of the modern software development processes that are associated with an agile approach, you can significantly mitigate the risk associated with a big bang transformation.

BIG-BANG TRANSFORMATION

# When to choose a big-bang transformation

To fully comprehend why this approach should be considered a last resort, it's worth identifying which factors might cause you to choose it for your legacy application transformation.

As mentioned previously, it should really only be considered once you have weighed up an iterative replacement or modernisation strategy, and you may decide these approaches are not appropriate for a number of reasons.

## Iteration would cost too much

One of the reasons you might resort to a big bang transformation is because you have concluded that both the iterative approaches would cost too much. As you consider iteratively replacing or modernising an application and start to sketch out how much engineering work would be involved, you may find that your preferred approaches are prohibitively expensive.

You might find that your application is of such critical business value that its transformation requires a near like-for-like replacement. The cost of building and then releasing such a system as a whole may be too high and finding an off-the-shelf replacement might make more sense.

If you are replacing an off-the-shelf application with another that must be released to the organisation in one go, you will need to consider a big bang transformation rather than taking an incremental approach. You could find ways to do things incrementally but development costs will increase and, if your budget is limited, a big bang transformation may be your only option.

You would never release custom software in one big bang because you will always develop it iteratively and therefore its release can be iterative too. As such, you should only ever use a big bang release when you are moving to off-the-shelf software, whether that be from custom software or another off-the shelf product.

## Data complexity

Data plays a major role in determining which transformation strategy is best and, as complexity increases, so does the likelihood of needing to resort to a big bang transformation.

Taking an iterative approach to transformation will require you to run two systems or more in parallel while functionality is gradually moved. If the data flow between old and new is relatively linear, you may well find that an iterative replacement or modernisation approach is possible. However, as soon as data flows start to zigzag around various systems, you might have to reconsider this as it may become too complex to be worthwhile.

You could build new functionality that wraps around old data, providing two views into the system. If the data can support both the old and the new, you can implement an incremental transformation strategy.

However, if not, you will find that a big-bang transformation is your only choice.

## Organisational constraints

Aside from data complexity and cost, you may find there are specific factors at play within your organisation that restrict your choice of strategies.

For example, deadlines brought about by licenses expiring or urgent policy changes may have to be considered. If you need to transform a specific and relatively simple application out quickly, a big bang transformation might make sense. By doing a quick analysis of the market, you might be able to identify an appropriate product and spend your time and effort on training rather than development.

Whatever your organisational situation though, resorting to a big bang transformation will usually involve weighing up complexity, cost, time and risk.

# Steps to take, decisions to make

Tread carefully if you choose to move forward with this type of transformation. You should rely on the important insights you have gathered in mapping your organisation and applications, as well as incorporating modern software techniques associated with agile development.

## Find the right product for you

Choosing the right product is an obvious but crucial step to take and you should refer back to the knowledge you have gathered about users to make the correct choice. You should also consider the application mapping you did to find the sort of products that will not become legacy technology.

For example, does the product have APIs and are these a core feature of its roadmap going forward? This matters so your data isn't locked away and inaccessible, if and when you decide to evolve your strategy further in future. Also, would this product involve getting locked into an expensive contract for a long time? If so, it's probably not the right option.

It's a good idea to begin any procurement process with a framework in place for judging how well suited a product might be to your needs. This can easily be developed beforehand from the research you've already done.

## Test it with users

You should also ask whether it's possible to do a demo of the product and to test it with users. You don't need to be using real data or a live environment at this point. It's about sitting with users, evaluating it with them and ensuring their needs are being met, just as you would if you were developing software yourself.

## Reduce risk with pre-production

Before you go live, you want to undertake further user research but with real data in a pre-production environment. This will be a valuable process to set up not just for your first release but all subsequent releases, as users will be able to evaluate changes in pre-production before they go live.

Having production parity between environments will help to reduce risk, so try to avoid having different versions of the application in different environments. You should automate data transfers from production to pre-production, obfuscate sensitive data and be able to reproduce pre-production environments automatically if a test migration goes wrong.

It's also a good idea to attempt a dummy run that doesn't affect production. Use continuous integration and delivery pipelines to attempt the deployment and migration, checking if any errors have occurred and also whether an automated roll out and roll back of the big bang is possible. Do this a few times to test it out and remove as many of the manual steps involved as possible.

## Form an iterative release plan

Think of your releases from a user perspective first and attempt to mitigate risks and disruptions to their daily routines in doing so. For example, can you turn a new system on and get people using it alongside the old system? Or, can you put one thing in the new system live first and release in iterations?

Consider adding users incrementally too, moving a small subset first to help mitigate risk. Attempting these steps out of hours, such as on the weekend, will allow you to attempt, iterate and try again, so as many issues as possible are eliminated.

You may choose a group of users based on a particular workflow in the application or a department in your organisation. Whatever you choose, always ensure user needs are driving your release pattern.

## Consider creating a playbook

You should always aim for automated scripts for your code documentation first. For example, when upgrading your system, you should test in a pre-production environment with realistic data and then release to live at the click of a button.

However, a playbook should also be considered. Anything that can't be automated should be included, as well as instructions for using the automated scripts. Documentation can quickly become stale if it's kept in a playbook and, if people use it, cause problems because they are following out of date instructions. Therefore it's always better to have people write the scripts than rely on the playbook.

## Plan your exit

Remember that you haven't found yourself implementing a big bang release as a result of perfect circumstances surrounding your legacy transformation. It was a compromise.

Therefore you should start to think about how you can iterate beyond it and plan your escape. Essentially, you have bought yourself some time with this strategy so that you can plan a proper iterative replacement later.

This is a stop gap and, once achieved, you should develop a plan for implementing sustainable technology in the future.

# Issues you may encounter

There's no doubt that a big bang transformation, which replaces incremental change with an all at once approach, is inherently risky and brings a number of issues with it. By identifying what they are, it will be easier to mitigate the risk they cause.

## Running parallel systems

If you can implement an iterative release plan as part of the steps you take in your big bang transformation, you will be running systems in parallel for a certain amount of time.

This may involve accessing data in a legacy application and exporting it in a format that can be imported into a new application, so that it's possible to run a new application in parallel with the existing one and share data between them. This approach enables you to switchover to the new application when you're ready or to revert back to the original application if the switchover goes wrong too.

To run the systems in parallel, you need to consider whether a) you have a team that is able to support them b) you can keep the data in sync and c) your licensing agreements allow it. If your answers to these questions are all yes, a strategy of running parallel applications makes sense. If not, this approach could land you with a mess of data that isn't synchronised.

## Building tomorrow's legacy today

As mentioned, your choice of a big bang strategy will have been your last resort, so you need to recognise this compromise, avoid the mistakes of the past and plan for an exit.

Vendors may encourage you down their path because it's in their best interests to do so. You should therefore consider whether your preference for their approach is in someway steered by any organisational naivety about what the correct technology choice is.

Ask yourself if you have considered the pain that a previous product caused your organisation's users and whether a vendor's offer is truly as user-friendly as they say it is. Also, remember that you are once again signing up to a license or subscription with a third-party that will cost you money and restrict your ability to change direction in future.

As mentioned, such a scenario could put you right back where you started from when you were weighing up the risks of legacy applications.

## Ongoing risk mitigation is key

Now you have a clear understanding of what each strategy entails, you should have enough information to decide which one to follow. Don't forget that the iterative approaches allow you to reevaluate and pivot as you progress, which is why a big bang transformation should be reserved as an option of last resort.

If you do decide a big bang transformation is the right approach for you, you need to be aware of the risks. In fact, ongoing risk mitigation is vital for every transformation strategy and something that you need to be constantly aware of.

# CHAPTER 3.5

## MITIGATING RISKS DURING LEGACY APPLICATION TRANSFORMATION

As you proceed with any legacy application transformation, you may encounter a range of different challenges that threaten to block your progress.

By preparing correctly, you will have spotted some of the potential issues early on. However, it would be wrong to assume that by doing this preparatory work, your transformation project will definitely run smoothly. These issues are all high risk enough to completely derail the project, so you need to be alert and deal with them as soon as they arise.

Many of them will pop up as you lift the lid and look inside an application but you shouldn't assume they will be entirely technical. The people and processes in your organisation could be the most likely things to scupper your plans, especially if you fail to engage them and bring them on the transformation journey with you.

## Keeping people aligned

It's important to recognise that legacy transformation is a team sport and that this team spirit needs to be sustained throughout.

Many organisations will be used to starting a big technology project with a boot up that brings together different areas of the organisation and feels engaging and collaborative for all involved. Unfortunately, this is often followed by the IT team going off to work away in the corner of the office (or worse, a basement) for weeks or months at a time.

All of sudden, you've gone from an aligned team that encompasses all areas of the organisation, to an isolated technology team that is expected to reveal a big bang transformation at some point in the future. This rarely ends well.

If you're not constantly engaging with different areas of your organisation, all sorts of issues can crop up. For example, if you're intending to integrate with a legacy system but haven't engaged with the team that operates it, you'll hit a blocker straight away. Equally, if you haven't got buy in from the service side of your organisation about a fundamental part of your strategy, you'll experience pushback when asking them to change.

It's also worth considering the role that organisational apathy can play. Have you really understood whether the business cares about legacy transformation, even if IT has the budget and the mandate for change? You might assume that your organisation will move as one once you have a key stakeholder on side but this ignores the myriad of parallel projects that might be of greater importance to other people.

You should also be prepared to see support wane if the project hits choppy waters. We've all heard the phrase "nobody got fired for buying IBM" and you need to be aware that this inherent risk aversion could manifest itself in people telling you "I told you so".

Keeping people aligned and constantly engaged with your legacy transformation is therefore crucial. If you don't, you risk the worst outcome - a rejection of what you have spent time and money building.

## Transforming processes

When you decide to modernise an application, it's important to remember that, if the application has been used for a long time, it will be at the heart of a whole range of business processes. Your organisational mapping will have helped you to understand these processes but have you thought about how they will need to change as the technology is transformed?

Failing to consider how processes need to change and incrementally adapt is particularly risky if you undertake an iterative modernisation or migration. Your organisation is likely to experience a situation where a new system needs to be used in parallel with an old system for some time. If you haven't considered how people will continue to do their jobs during this period, it could derail your entire project.

Rather than be surprised by this change of behaviour, you should engage with the different areas that are affected in order to plan how to keep disruption to a minimum. Implementing technology and training people how to use it as you go is crucial, so you should be thinking about what communications need to be sent out and what training sessions need to be scheduled in.

## Accessing data

When it comes to technical risks, most revolve around data.

The first big issue to consider is access, whether that be on-premise access or data centre access, as you will need to connect into the local network or the data centre network. You should have flagged these issues during the mapping of applications but things will inevitably have been missed.

These are unknown unknowns that you want to turn into known unknowns as soon as possible, so you can then resolve them entirely. Connections into third-party systems are likely to be a headache and network or authentication issues can be expected. It's therefore a good idea to start by making limited early investigations of the data and scraping any data you can before you start developing.

When dealing with data centres, you might find that you need to go through an assurance process that checks whether your organisation is competent enough. An example could be ISO 10007, which ensures that people with access can handle data properly. Be aware that any form filling or assessments could delay the transformation and potentially result in a loss of confidence in the project amongst key stakeholders.

You should also consider the implications of having to deal with secure data. You need to understand where the data lives and why, what encryption is used and who can access it. If you're planning to pull production data into a local network, this might not be allowed.

Finally, it's also important to understand any firewalls or IP restrictions that might stop you connecting to a database, application or API.

## Interacting with APIs

Identifying that a legacy application has an API can be something of a double edged sword. Having an established and hopefully documented way of accessing data from the application is obviously beneficial but it's often not as simple as that.

APIs usually worsen as an application ages and you'll probably find that there are insufficient APIs in place. You may find that there's a way to get the data out but it could be impractical or inefficient. The API might be slow or broken. If it's one that a vendor provides for a piece of off-the-shelf software, you may find it has a bug that they're not willing to fix. If you find that the API is insufficient or that there's no API to interact with at all, you'll need to work out how you are going to pull data out of a legacy application.

Accessing data and testing how you can use it in a modernised application always requires you to understand exactly how the business uses the data in the first place. If you don't, your work could have unintended consequences. Furthermore, if there's no documentation to explain these data structures and flows, you will need to factor in time and effort for reverse engineering these processes.

## Using poor quality data

Even if you can access data and use APIs to pull it from a legacy application, your transformation could still be affected if the underlying data quality is poor.

There are all sorts of reasons why you might describe the data you find as poor. It could be relationally inconsistent, littered with duplications or just plain wrong. There's also the fact that some data, such as contact details, can become less and less accurate over time if not kept up-to-date.

All of these issues need to be identified as quickly as possible, so you can establish a process for fixing errors, cleaning the data and sanity checking the changes that have been. This could be time consuming and doing it early on will help to ensure it doesn't block progress.

## Stay alert to the risks

As no application is the same, the risks you need to mitigate are not either. The preparatory work you did to map your organisation and applications will have gone a long way to helping you mitigate any risks that could occur once you start your legacy transformation.

However diligent you have been though, there will always be things that were missed. You need to stay alert to these dangers and deal with them as soon as you sense any of them starting to appear. By doing so, you'll ensure the path is clear for the important first step of embarking on a pilot.

# CHAPTER 3.6

# INITIATING A PILOT AT THE START OF YOUR LEGACY TRANSFORMATION

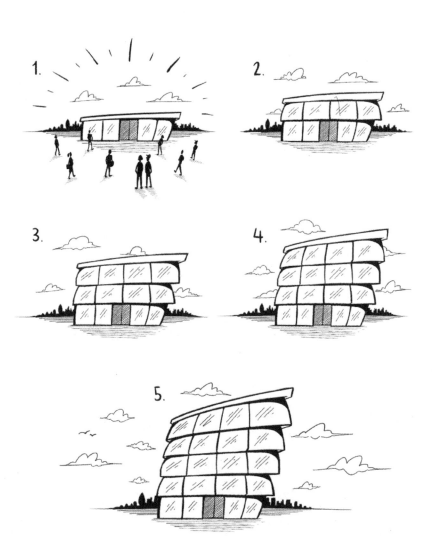

The first meaningful steps you take in your transformation will always feel uncertain, however much solid preparatory work you have done beforehand. Modernising legacy applications isn't easy and the danger that an unknown issue might derail your project never fully disappears. However, by initiating a pilot at the start, you can go a long way to reducing these risks.

A pilot is a first step in the implementation of your chosen legacy transformation strategy that solves a real problem for your organisation. You should be able to deliver your pilot quickly and release it to users within weeks.

By solving a problem decisively you will build momentum in your transformation. The pilot will help you to pull people into or along with the project as it progresses. It can also allow you to prove a method or process you have proposed as part of your transformation strategy.

A pilot has a number of additional benefits beyond risk reduction. It enables you to build momentum and helps you to pull people into or along with the project as it progresses. It can also allow you to prove a method or process you have proposed as part of your transformation strategy.

Most significantly though, it allows you to start delivering. Up to now, you will have undertaken a lot of important research and planning. Now is the time to start actioning what you have learnt and begin transforming not just your applications but also how your organisation delivers and benefits from sustainable technology.

## Why embark on a pilot?

A pilot can help to mitigate risks, build momentum and prove a method. It's particularly useful at the start of your transformation journey because it allows you to tread carefully as you build confidence.

The extensive mapping work you did at the start of the project, particularly the mapping of applications, will have helped you immensely in identifying the risks you must consider and the blockers you might face. These may have guided your decisions around which application to modernise first and which strategy to choose. However, some risks will not have disappeared entirely and others may have been missed. Embarking on a pilot is a great way of mitigating risks in legacy transformation.

Pilots allow you to prove a method early on, tackling a tricky but significant issue as soon as possible. They can not only help you move forward but also build momentum in your organisation. The tangible success of a pilot can silence naysayers, build confidence within your team and even open up further funding if you need to prove a business case. To ensure your pilot has this kind of effect, you must ensure it is set up in the right way.

## What makes a great pilot?

A successful pilot always provides value to the organisation. It doesn't need to be a revolutionary development though and can just be about changing a small piece of functionality or workflow in a previous application. What's most important is that you focus on a discrete slice of the problem rather than trying to boil the ocean.

In the case of an iterative modernisation, your overriding objective for the transformation will be to change and improve an existing application. Therefore your pilot should be designed to add new value and prove you are doing more than was possible before. If you want to move your technology stack forward, your pilot might focus on moving onto the latest version of a programming language, software library or other dependency. Alternatively, you may choose to create a feature that demonstrates your ability to respond to new policy changes.

For an iterative replacement, your transformation may be focused on pulling data from a legacy application and showing you can do something new and worthwhile with it. In this situation, your pilot might focus on proving you can get over the hump of a tricky data integration as a first step. It might involve pulling data out and showing how it can be used in a replacement that provides better functionality. If your replacement is a SaaS product, the pilot might aim to do one thing better than before, such as automating a manual process.

For big bang transformations, your whole approach should be focused on derisking the process. A good use of a pilot might be to move a subset of users first. You may choose to limit the roll out to users who perform a certain role or work in a particular department. By introducing this sort of iterative and incremental change at the pilot stage, you'll be helping to mitigate the chances of things going wrong when a full switchover occurs.

# How to shape your pilot

The first and most important step is to build a problem statement that needs to be addressed. You should ensure that it delivers a tangible business outcome for your organisation rather than existing as some sort of isolated research and development project. This is important because, by adding value, you will build advocacy for the transformation project.

One of the most important things to get right when designing your pilot is its scope. Identifying goals and KPIs for the pilot will help you to get the scope right. Start by knowing what you want to change and then direct your efforts towards moving the metric you use to measure that change.

Once you have your problem statement, goals and KPIs in place, you need to form a team for the pilot. As mentioned previously, legacy transformation is a team sport and your pilot is the perfect opportunity to get that team working together. The team needs to be representative of the entire organisation, so the pilot can build momentum for the wider project.

With your problem statement established and your team in place, it's time to build. Keep in mind that, while your problem statement provides a goal to aim for, it should actually break down into lots of small steps. This means your team needs to be building in short, iterative bursts that prove something of significance, before moving straight onto the next thing to build and prove.

This is not a time for people working with their headphones on and their heads down. They need to be showcasing regularly and reporting back on a daily and weekly basis. It's important to start your pilot with this iterative process in mind, rather than with one big release goal at the end.

## Making a success of your pilot

Confidence will build naturally if you can clearly communicate what you are attempting to validate and the metrics you are monitoring to test the pilot's success or failure. Even failure means learning and, because you're iterating in small slices, it's not expensive or bad to fail. You should make it clear how the pilot is designed to help the team fail fast and improve.

Also, consider involving individuals who can spread the word once the pilot is complete. For example, if you are attempting to modernise an application that is used by a large department, recruit a small cohort of pioneering staff to take part first.

These individuals can become advocates for the transformation as it progresses beyond a pilot. You might choose to include someone you've won favour with early on or someone whose career is linked to the success of the transformation. You might plump for someone simply because they are keen to get involved.

What's important to remember is that you want people who are enthusiastic about what you are proposing. If you are trying to build confidence in a legacy team or to gradually introduce new skills that will transform how your organisation operates, you want these enthusiastic advocates at the core of your team.

This is also why regular, ongoing reporting is so important during the pilot. You need your team to be feeding back to the business as early and often as possible, so they can see your successes and flag any risks that pop up.

## Progressing beyond your pilot

Once you're into the process of building, iterating and proving, your pilot will generate the momentum your transformation really needs. Ideally, progress has been made, risks have been mitigated and confidence has been built in your team and the wider organisation.

Most significantly though, your pilot should have started to embed some of the key skills and techniques that you can take forward as you progress. Foremost amongst these is the iterative process you have followed by tackling a discrete problem.

You need to continue this iterative approach on an ongoing basis, biting off another chunk of work, assessing it against your risk appetite and getting your team's teeth stuck into it. Before long, you'll be so used to delivering sustainable technology you'll hardly notice how significant your transformation has been!

# CHAPTER 4

## FROM LEGACY APPLICATIONS TO SUSTAINABLE TECHNOLOGY

When you begin your transformation journey, you know your legacy applications pose a significant risk to your organisation. One of the most important lessons you learn as you modernise these applications is that you can never let that situation occur again.

This is what it means to truly and definitely move away from legacy applications. It is not just about modernising your technology estate. It's about transforming your entire operating model into one that is tuned to deliver sustainable technology.

To achieve this, you need to focus on three key areas - continuous modernisation, ongoing maintainability and a new model for funding technology.

## Continuous modernisation

Regardless of whether you decided to transform one or more legacy applications at the outset, the process of continuous modernisation needs to become part of your regular working practices.

You need to constantly assess and reassess the status of your applications so you have a regularly updated view of what modernisations need to be made. You can achieve this by utilising the techniques you adopted in mapping your applications. The attributes you recorded should be monitored to ensure that legacy applications don't become an issue for your organisation once again.

When performing these regular reassessments, you should also look at your priorities to see if and how they've changed. You may find that your first experience of transforming a legacy application has given you confidence to go further with another application than you thought possible or that it has limited your ambitions because of the obstacles you hit.

Your organisation's priorities will undoubtedly change too. It's not uncommon for a legacy application transformation to take six months or longer, during which time strategic goals can shift and user expectations change. An important part of your regular reassessments should be examining whether an application continues to provide value for your organisation. If it does not, it should be retired.

What you're aiming to do is set up procedures that ensure your modernisation becomes business as usual and periods of transformation become a thing of the past. This is where DevOps culture plays an important role. If you have previously operated on the basis that the development team releases software and the operations team runs it, this needs to change. DevOps is about the same team building and running software, and is vital for ensuring modernisation continues.

## Ongoing maintainability

If you have spent six months or more transforming a legacy application, you don't want to keep doing the same thing again and again. This is why ongoing maintainability matters.

An important part of maintainability is keeping things up-to-date. If you're using a SaaS product, a high quality vendor will be fixing bugs and continually upgrading the software. Therefore it's worth keeping an eye on whether your vendor follows these processes.

For installed software, keeping things up-to-date means ensuring you are always using the latest stable release. For developed software, it means monitoring a range of languages, libraries and other elements to make sure you are using the latest versions. One of the best ways to do this is by scheduling in an audit of all dependencies to recur on a monthly basis. If nothing has changed, you shouldn't consider this audit a waste of time. However, when updates are required, they should be scheduled into development sprints.

Keeping the age of technology low can be done fairly easily if you set up this sort of constant monitoring. It needs to be regular but can also be relatively light touch. In this way, you can ensure no security vulnerabilities occur because of update gaps. One way to think about it is like paying off your credit card on a monthly basis. By doing so, you avoid a big shock at the end of the year and the same is true with software.

To make maintenance easier, you should employ the new ways of working you will have introduced during your transformation journey. For example, continuous integration and delivery (CI/CD) pipelines and automated testing will help improve maintainability on an ongoing basis. You can even run automated and semi-automated dependency upgrades and checks as part of your pipeline.

A DevOps culture will also play its part, as the team that builds the software is then made responsible not only for running it but also fixing any bugs. This is particularly important for developed software and you need to be explicit about these responsibilities.

## A new funding model

You'll find it almost impossible to sustain any of these optimised ways of working if you do not back them up with the funding they require.

If you're following the correct path of asking your technology team to take on added responsibility for continuously maintaining and modernising software, you need to make sure it has the capacity to do so. In many cases, this will mean investment is required to grow the team.

Getting yourself out of the mindset that once software is running it is 'done' also involves shifting how you think about paying for applications. You will have spent a chunk of capital expenditure on transforming your applications up to this point. This will have allowed you to get out of expensive ransom contracts with big IT vendors, so you can fund your applications at a lower ongoing cost over the course of their lifetimes. As capital expenditure is replaced by operational expenditure, technology costs move from your organisation's balance sheet to its profit and loss statement.

# Delivering sustainable technology

Keep in mind that, simply by following the steps we have outlined for modernising legacy applications, you have already moved your organisation onto the path of delivering sustainable technology.

By prioritising continuous modernisation and ongoing maintainability, as well as the funding required to achieve them both, you'll continue to make progress. It's also a good idea to surround yourself with like-minded organisations, suppliers and experts who can keep you on track and support the ongoing transformation of your entire operating model.

If you do, you will not only be enabling your team to embrace and adapt to change but also to deliver sustainable technology long into the future.

# About Made Tech

Made Tech are public sector technology delivery experts. We provide Digital, Data and Technology services across the UK market.

We help public sector leaders to modernise legacy applications and working practices, accelerate digital service delivery, drive smarter decisions with data and enable improved technology skills within teams.

Founded in 2012, we grew by helping startups to build products fast using lean and agile principles. Since 2016, we have been helping public sector organisations to adopt these skills, capabilities and ways of working to deliver better outcomes for citizens.

Find us at www.madetech.com

Printed in Great Britain
by Amazon

82977897R00108